# MORE
# steeple
# stories

compiled by
**OREN ARNOLD**

✠

**KREGEL PUBLICATIONS**
Grand Rapids, Michigan 49503

Printed in the United States of America

# Acknowledgments

*Given the chance, any honest sinner likes to Drop Names. I am no exception. Wherefore, acknowledgment is gratefully given to the following saintly celebrities who have "told me their best ones" while we broke bread together: President Richard M. Nixon, Dr. Billy Graham, Dr. Norman Vincent Peale, Sen. Barry Goldwater, Bishop Fulton J. Sheen, DeWitt Wallace, Everett Smith, Dr. George Crane, Sen. Mark Hatfield, Dick Van Dyke, Abigail Van Buren and Sen. Carl Hayden.*

— Oren Arnold

# Preface

What's funny about church? Everything! Humor develops spontaneously, no matter what is done or who does it. After years of writing regular pages of humor in several church magazines, I get thousands of reports from secretaries, singers, sextons, and assuredly from ministers. Many of these are true incidents, and wherever I could do so without causing embarrassment, I have used the best of these in this book, with real names and places. A few names were changed "to protect the innocent."

But the apocryphal stories, jokes, puns, quips and yarns are even more numerous and delightful. Those chosen for *More Steeple Stories* may be the best yet. Items that obviously are not true carry fictitious names, such as those of our old friends Dr. Saddlie Thredbaire, Sebe Cornstalk, and Dunkle Pedunkle.

Certainly we would hurt nobody's feelings in these pages. This book is offered only with the deepest reverence. As carefully stated in *Steeple Stories of Saints and Sinners,* God made us in His image, and most of us feel this includes a sense of humor. Humor is irreverent only when we laugh derisively, never when we laugh in wholesome fun, never when we laugh at ourselves. Keep in mind what we are told in Proverbs 15:15 : ". . . he that is of a merry heart hath a continual feast."

# Contents

# 1.
# Amusing Anecdotes

*In Hollywood one day, Bishop Fulton J. Sheen dropped into a little wayside cafe. The pert waitress did not recognize her distinguished customer. Accustomed to movie actors and extras coming in during rehearsal breaks fully costumed, she barely glanced at His Eminence in his flowing red robe.*

*She just paused a moment at his table and said, "Okay, Robin Hood, what'll it be for you?"*

✠

A new Methodist pastor had just come to America from northern Europe. The good man was very earnest, but his congregation struggled to understand his dialect, and he in turn struggled to understand their American idiom. One day the district superintendent was visiting, and the pastor's sermon was going especially well. Even so, he seemed a bit self-conscious, so near the end of the sermon the superintendent whispered a suggestion that the pastor "open the doors of the church." It is a customary way of inviting sinners to join.

The good preacher, although astonished, left the rostrum, walked down front and opened the doors, opened the side doors, came on back and finished his sermon — on a near-zero day in January!

*This story is told of two famous personages:*

*In London during World War II, the Nazi planes were blasting everything in sight with bombs. The Archbishop ran to Sir Winston Churchill for advice. "Bolster everything with sandbags," ordered Sir Winston. "Prop up everything. But no matter how many close hits the Nazis may make, I feel certain the cathedral will come through unharmed."*

*"Perhaps so, close hits," agreed the jittery Archbishop. "But what if they score a direct hit on my place, even while I'm in there?"*

*"In that case, my dear Archbishop, you will be forced to regard it as a summons."*

✠

Fate overtook Rev. Jonathan P. Devore in his southern church one Sunday, just as he reached the climax of his sermon. Beloved "Dr. Jon" stepped from behind his pulpit to emphasize a moral point. He walked to the front of the rostrum, raised both arms high and shouted, "Drop off the things that bind you." He meant, of course, their sins.

But at that exact moment his suspenders gave way, and his too-loose black pants fell to the floor!

✠

*Allegedly, any mouse that hangs around a church is a victim of malnutrition and financial deprivation. But the allegations aren't always true. The last mouse I saw in church was a fat and prosperous looking mouse who had joined the 1,200 well-fed members of the congregation shepherded by the then-distinguished minister, Charles Samuel Poling, D.D.*

*Dr. Poling was the soul of dignity. He had an ascetic's face; he somehow gave the impression that he not only loved the Lord, but was in intimate, hourly contact with Him. Thus services in his church were always reverent.*

*Even so, this Sunday morning midway through the sermon, he paused at the height of an oratorical phrase to stare at a creature that had climbed up the side of his pulpit!*

*One cannot just pick up a book and clobber a mouse with 1,200 or so worshipers looking on. What can one do about a live Mickey Mouse sitting up on one's pulpit in the middle of one's sermon?*

*Nothing!*

*Dr. Poling did it.*

*After services Dr. Poling and two caretakers set four traps and waited confidently for Mickey's demise. But he enjoyed church too much. The traps rested all week, untouched. Come next Sunday, Mickey was back with assorted kinsmen.*

*If Dr. Poling's scholarly discourses that season lacked some element of perfection, this went unnoticed. Church attendance was never better, enthusiasm never higher. Even the front pews were filled; indeed, they filled earliest of all.*

*There is no dramatic climax. Nobody ever knew what became of Mickey. One Sunday he and his henchmen were there, next Sunday they weren't. Perhaps they began attending services at the Baptist church, nearby.*

✠

One day the Reverend William H. Hubbard was preaching in Auburn, New

York. Through the side door wobbled a man obviously so drunk he couldn't tell north from east, and he managed to get up there and sit down near the preacher — without Dr. Hubbard seeing him.

But as the preacher made important point after point in his sermon, the newcomer would endorse it with a loud "Yea, yea, you tell 'em, parson!"

After a few such endorsements, Dr. Hubbard with some dignity did turn to the man and say, "You must stop making so much noise."

The drunk shouted back, "Who's making a noise?"

✝

*In Seattle, Dr. Blank, a man of dignity and one much loved, suffered a minor accident just two minutes before church time. A quantity of water was spilled down the side of his trousers.*

*In the interest of time, he quickly shucked off the trousers and put on his heavy robe, which he would have worn anyhow. He reasoned that he could approach his pulpit from the side and nobody would notice an absence of trousers cuffs down below.*

*It worked out just that way, too. He gave a fine sermon, there was good music, everything was perfect. So after service he went back down to the robe room, whistling softly in satisfaction, his mind "somewhere else" as he reported, because he had forgotten all about having removed his trousers.*

*With sopranos and contraltos all removing their choir robes, he removed his robe and hung it up, then blithely started back upstairs to greet people,*

*unaware of his hanging shirt tail and bare legs.*
*Until a soprano screamed a high C of alarm!*

✠

The Rev. Phil Gregory, a Congregational minister, noted that his sermon manuscripts were stacking up on him and getting in the way. So he asked his secretary to get a cardboard box from downtown and store them away. She did. Next week he found them on a closet shelf, in a liquor box labeled with perhaps insulting accuracy — VERY DRY.

✠

*In Houston, Texas, Mrs. Stella Blanck, a church organist and Sunday school teacher, appeared before a judge on a charge of making an illegal left turn while driving. She pleaded her own case, and in the process said that she was trying to raise $200 for her church. Kindly Judge Levy dismissed the charges.*

*Touched by her appeal for church money, even the prosecuting attorney handed her a $5 bill. Then the arresting officers each contributed. All that impressed the judge again, so he reached over the bench and handed her five dollars. She almost cried in her gratitude as she left the courthouse.*

*She was back in five minutes. She had a ticket for over-parking.*

*Judge Levy dismissed that one too. "She has the Lord on her side," he explained.*

✠

Many years ago a small Christmas tree in a small-town church was decorated with real candles, and all the good folk had gathered to celebrate. But a tom-cat had also joined the celebration and became entranced by the tree's glitter. . . . He climbed the tree, toppled it, and flames started. An alert deacon grabbed a hat, dipped water from the baptistry and threw it toward the small fire in the pine branches.

Unfortunately, the Rev. Elroy Hardcastle had ducked down at that moment, trying to extinguish the fire with his coat. He, not the tree, got the full splash of water.

"Oh, Henry, for goodness' sakes!" cried the deacon's wife. *She*, the efficiency expert, grabbed the hat and ran to refill it.

You guessed it — in the melee, Henry got *this* hat full of water smack in the face!

Meanwhile the preacher had gotten to his feet, and now *he* grabbed the hat, ran for water, ran back and threw it — all over Mrs. Henry the efficiency gal! Little or none ever got on the blaze.

Happily, the blaze didn't amount to much anyway, and nobody was hurt. The tree was righted, the ornaments reset, the children again made happy. The steeple people gave prayers of thanks, sang carols, exchanged gifts, and went on home.

That was more than sixty years ago in a Texas town. The children present that night now have grandchildren who enjoy hearing the true story.

✠

One Sunday in Rockford, Illinois, a mouse trotted down the center aisle of a church. Mrs. Weems saw it first, and screamed. Then Mrs. Bolliger saw it, and screamed. In sixty seconds the congregation was in an uproar. The preacher stopped his sermon, but that didn't stop the mouse. It ran on up the rostrum steps, up the front of the pulpit, and sat up on its hind legs, facing the preacher.

The minister rolled his sermon manuscript and swung it — WHACK!

The mouse dodged, ran down the pulpit, up the side of a pew, and sat up this time facing Mrs. Mc-Swain. By this time an usher was on the job — or trying to be. He swung a hymnal as a club, missed the mouse, swung again and knocked Mr. Mouse into Mrs. McSwain's thick fur collar. Mickey burrowed in there for safety.

Mrs. McSwain refused to panic. She simply got up, walked out the side door with an usher, and there helped him demolish the mouse.

✠

*Beloved Uncle Dooley Watson couldn't write or read, but he loved to go to Sunday school. Because he couldn't read, he always sat in the next to the last row, so that a friend right behind him could whisper the Scripture words and Uncle Dooley would repeat them aloud.*

*One day he repeated, "The Lord said unto Moses," and paused, awaiting his whispered prompting. But the light was dim that day, and Uncle Dooley's hand was obscuring the friend's view of the Good Book. The friend whispered something hurriedly, and Uncle Dooley went on with it: ". . . The Lord said unto Moses, get your silly hand out of the light."*

✠

'Twas the night before Christmas. The dean of Trinity Cathedral telephoned his parishioner, Ellis Fisher, a heating expert: "Please come and check our furnace, Ellis, to be sure we have heat for the evening service." He'd be glad to, Ellis said.

Fisher came to the cathedral alley entrance with his father-in-law, Dr. Moss, on their way home at 6 P.M. They walked downstairs. A brilliant 300-watt light blinded them, but they checked the furnace controls and made sure all was well. "Let's just go up through the sanctuary and make sure the heat is coming through," Ellis suggested.

Still blinded by that light, Ellis came out back of the pulpit. Only two candles glowed dimly in the great auditorium. Ellis held up a hand. "Already hot as hades in here, Doc," he yelled.

"Doggone if it ain't," Doc agreed, loud tone.

Fumbling in the dim light, they came down the altar steps into the main aisle. Doc, leading, shouted back again, "Let's get out of this sweat shop. No place for a fat man."

"You'd better stop eating Christmas cake." That from Ellis, very loud. Then — *"Doc!"*

*"Ellis!"*

The two dignified Episcopalians ran out the front door, hurried around to their car, hurried home, and avoided church for weeks. There in the sanctuary their eyes had gradually adjusted, and they saw twenty or more worshipers already kneeling in prayer!

✠

*In an Iowa church the Methodists have an annual "Layman's Sunday" when selected laymen give the pulpit messages. One Sunday the preacher chose three men and told them they had just six minutes each, to speak.*

*But you know how that is. Sure enough, the first one got up and spoke for 24 minutes. However, there was some interruption, which most of the con-*

*gregation frankly welcomed. His topic was "Alcoholism," which he decried with tedious statistics and such. All the while an innocent little girl down front who had a bad case of hiccoughs kept loudly exploding, "HIC . . . HIC . . . HIC!"*

✠

The Rev. Frank Prucia never liked to have his services disturbed, and his family knew it. But one morning a little three-year-old girl ambled up onto the platform and began to dance around, right in the middle of his sermon.

He tried valiantly to ignore her, but the worshipers couldn't. So — his own five-year-old daughter, sitting down front and indignant for him now, ran up, grabbed the naughty little girl and roundly spanked her, with several hundred approving worshipers gleefully witnessing.

✠

Many incidents become legends, living on through the years. This old favorite originated in Oban, Scotland, when a big poster in front of the Presbyterian Church there startled the Scots. The poster read:
Sermon — "What Is Hell Like?"
Come and hear our choir.

✠

*Then there is the story about the rather pitiable 17-year-old boy with long hair, beard, and a two-weeks' fragrance, and a cynical attitude toward life. Somehow he was lured into a "nice" church party and during the evening he challenged the choir director by asking, "Honestly now, is there a God?"*

**15**

*The astute choir director tactfully made the young cynic promise to attend church the next day to hear the choir sing Handel's matchless* Messiah. *He really went, too, and wouldn't you know it — the church bulletin that Sunday had been proofread carelessly. The printed title over one of the great concluding choruses read:*

"Hallelujah, the Lord God Omnipotent Resigneth!"

*The whimsy there was just enough to break down the last bit of reserve in the young cynic. He not only joined the choir, he later joined the church. He had discovered that church folk were "human" just like he.*

✠

One Easter morning, a large sanctuary was crowded. The balcony was full too when a well-known Deputy Sheriff crept in to worship. Deputy Blank didn't get to church often and felt ill at ease, and there was no seat left for him anyway. So he told the usher he'd just sit on the top balcony step.

At that moment the preacher started his prayer, and Deputy Blank leaned over to bow in reverence. That leaning was just enough to dislodge a pearl-handled revolver from his shoulder holster, where it had been out of sight.

Now it struck the top balcony step, went *clump, bump, thump, bump, CRASH*, step-by-step down the balcony steps and onto the wooden railing twenty feet below, while appalled worshipers looked spellbound.

Deputy Blank, chagrin showing on his face, retrieved his gun, hurried out of church, and in eleven years has not returned.

# 2.
# Dead Ends

*Hiram's third wife died. Mary Cornstalk said to her husband, "Sebe, are you going to attend the funeral of Hiram's wife?"*

*Sebe considered at length, and finally ruled, "No, I ain't, honey. I want to Hiram's first wife's funeral, I went to his second wife's funeral, but I ain't going to the funeral for this'n."*

*"Why not?" Mary demanded.*

*"Well, sweetheart, it just don't seem right, me acceptin' all of Hiram's invitations, and never havin' nothing like that to invite him back to."*

✝

Dr. Hall called on the sorrowing colonel. "I came by to express my deepest sympathy, Sir. I just read in the morning paper that you buried your wife yesterday."

"Harrumph, yes. Yes, of course we buried her. Had to — she died, you know."

✝

The pastor had been called; it was an emergency, the woman on the phone said. When he got there he asked what had happened.

"An explosion," said the wife. "Henry struck a match to see if he had any gasoline in the gas tank."

"Struck a match! Why, I should think that would be the last thing on earth he would do!"

"It was."

When one hillbilly husband died, his wife hauled the casket to the railroad and said to the ticket agent, "I want a ticket to Dallas for me, and another one for my husband's body."

"That's odd," said the agent. "Why a ticket for him?"

"Well, in Dallas is a lot of his kinfolks. It'll be a lot cheaper if I ship him there for them to look at and bawl, than if I phone them and let 'em all come traipsin' over to my house where I'll have to feed and house 'em for a week."

✠

*Did we say something about the Scots being Scotch? Well, Mrs. McTavish had been rushed to the hospital. After a long day her minister called Mr. Mac at his home and reported that the good woman had passed on.*

*Did Scotty then rush to the hospital first thing? No! Scotty went first to the kitchen and said to the maid, "Lisbeth, ye need boil only one egg for breakfast tomorrow."*

✠

Seems that an actor famed as a tragedian lost his wife, and at graveside he broke down in a most heart-rending display of grief. On the way home, the pastor sought to comfort him. "My, my, Henry, you certainly were weeping there at the cemetery."

"Oh that was nothing, really," said the modest actor. "You should have seen me at the funeral parlor."

✠

*Plump Mrs. Meeker was worried. "Henry," she began, "if I die, and you should ever marry again, promise me that you* will never allow your next wife to wear my clothes."

"Of course I promise, Henrietta. And besides — they wouldn't fit her."

✠

Consider poor Joe Blow. He joined a funeral procession in his car, figuring he could roll through a red light and save time. He got through, all right, but when he glanced in his rear view mirror he saw a motorcycle cop in the procession, just behind him. Poor Joe had to stay there all the way to Resthaven Cemetery, eight miles out of his way!

✠

There are times when we can feel a crumb of pity even for a thief. Envision the consternation of this one.

Joe and Jane Jones were motoring across country with Jane's mother in the car also. Sadly, Mom was stricken with an illness when they were in the Nevada wilderness, and she suddenly died.

No town or help was in sight, so Joe and his wife wrapped the body in a blanket, tied it on top of the car in the luggage rack, and hastened on. At length they came to Las Vagas, and stopped at the first building they recognized as a church.

"Let's go in here and ask the preacher what to do," Joe suggested.

The good parson was kind, and said they had done the right thing. He talked a bit to comfort them, offered a prayer, then said he would accompany them to the local mortuary. But when they came outside again, somebody had stolen the car and all that was on it!

The vicar's wife died suddenly, and he was devastated. He didn't want to conduct services on Sunday, and therefore he wired his bishop, wording it thus:

"Regret to inform you that I have just lost my wife; please send me a substitute for this week-end."

✠

Scotty McPherson went sadly into the newspaper office and asked the proprietor, "How much do ye charge for printing a funeral notice?"

Replied the printer, "It's 75 cents an inch."

"Dear, dear me!" murmured Scotty, frowning. "And my poor brother-in-law was over six feet tall!"

✠

*The undertaker telephoned the preacher and said, "We would like you to conduct the funeral service for J. P. Wilson."*

*"Why, for goodness' sakes!" exclaimed the pastor. "Did Mr. Wilson die?"*

*Said the bored undertaker, "Do you think his family would be conducting rehearsals?"*

✠

Ike had been a truly bad man — one of the roughest, toughest outlaws of the Old West, mean and vicious. When he was shot in a saloon brawl the local folk took him out for the burying; the preacher offered a prayer, and invited his friends to say any words in eulogy. But all the folk just stared; nobody said a word for a long three or four minutes.

Finally one old man who had grown up with Ike stepped forward. "Friends," said he, "as a kid, Ike used to shoot a mighty good game of marbles. I remember once he won 25 marbles, playin' after school."

✠

The Gate opened, the good pastor walked in. Peter said, "Here is your golden harp."

Said the all-American capitalistic parson, "How much is the first payment?"

✠

A proud Texan died and arrived at the Pearly Gates. St. Peter looked out, recognized him, sighed a little, and said: "Well, okay, Tex, come on in. But you won't like it."

✠

*Two of his parishioners were in the news one morning, and the minister was discussing them with his wife. "I knew them both as boys," said he. "One was a handsome chap, very clever. The other was plain, steady, and hard working. The clever one was left behind in life's race, but the hard worker prospered and left his young widow with a fortune of a half million dollars. It is a great moral."*

*"It sure is," agreed his wife. "I heard this morning that the clever brother is going to marry the widow."*

✠

This was in the town pharmacy, and the men there were discussing prize fighting. A newcomer said, "Well, I can say one thing, I have boxed many of the best men in this entire county, and not a one of them hit me back." Then he walked out.

"Who was that?" the others asked the pharmacist.

"He's the town's biggest undertaker."

✠

*In an old soldiers' home the minister had just conducted a funeral service. No eulogy was read, because no information was available, and no kinfolk showed. But at the end, one elderly widow of a soldier said to her friend, "If I hadn't a knowed who it was, I wouldn't of knowed who it was."*

✠

Parson Brown heard over the rural party telephone that Alex McTavish was ill with a high fever.

Two days later he managed to walk the five miles to the McTavish farm.

"Mighty sorry to hear that Alex is sick," said he to Mrs. Mac at the front door. "What is his temperature today, ma'am?"

"Can't rightly say," she declared primly. "He died yesterday."

✠

Both his wife and his pastor had despaired of saving the soul of poor, sinning Samuel Smith. Finally Sam died. At the last opening of the casket, the pastor prayed, but the widow looked sorrowfully at the remains and said, "Oh, me, Sammy, I sholy hopes you has gone where I expects you ain't."

# 3.
# Kid Stuff

*Little Louella came into the kitchen and asked, "Mommy, is it true that we came from dust and will return to dust?"*

*"Certainly, darling. That's what The Bible tells us. Why?"*

*"Well," said Lou, "I just now looked under my bed, and somebody under there is either going or coming."*

✠

"What can you tell me about Aaron?" the Sunday-school teacher asked her class of juniors.

After a moment of cogitation, one lad said, "Well, most likely his name was the first one in the telephone book."

✠

The need for missionaries of course is great, and the Sunday-school teacher was trying to get this fact across. She told a story about a poor African. Deep in the jungle he broke his arm. He was taken to Dr. Schweitzer's hospital, where for the first time he learned about Christianity.

"In a few days," she concluded her story, "his arm was well, and he was returned safely to his native village. Now, how could that poor man learn more about Christianity?"

The hoped-for and expected answer didn't come. Silence held the children for several seconds, then Jasper Smith finally held up a hand and said, "I know — he could break his other arm."

A celebrated comedian had several guests in his home one evening. The children, as usual, were a part of the party, and were taking active part in the conversation.

"Do you young people attend church regularly?" one guest asked them.

"Oh, yes, sir," replied a child. "We are all Catholics in this home."

At which point the youngest put in, "All except Daddy. He's a comedian."

✠

*The pastor, walking toward his church one Sabbath morn met young Mary Lou Wilson and began chatting with her. "I am happy that you are going to Sunday school today, my child," said he. "What do you expect to learn this morning?"*

*Replied Mary Lou eagerly, "The date of the Sunday-school picnic."*

✠

The Sunday-school lesson concerned the Good Samaritan. Teacher asked, "Why did the priest and the Levite pass by on the other side?"

Butch Brown replied: "Because the poor man had already been robbed."

✠

"Who," asked the Sunday-school teacher, "can tell me the meaning of the term, 'the quick and the dead?'"

Young David Detwiler had prompt answer: "The quick are the people who get out of the way of cars, the dead are the ones that don't."

Our pastor must learn to enunciate more clearly. One young girl reported to her mother that he said he would accept her letter of transfer from any "Eve and jelly" church.

✠

*Now consider the little girl whose teacher asked, "Can you tell us who Joan of Arc was?" This sweetling replied, "She must have been Noah's wife."*

✠

Mrs. Grandiose Gotmillion, a haughty matron, called in a huff and said to the minister, "Dr. Meeker, did you tell my little girl in Sunday school that I was a great rusty cat?"

Appalled, Dr. Meeker reassured her. "Why, no indeed! What I *said* was, 'Mrs. Gotmillion is a great aristocrat.'"

✠

The sanctuary in one big church in Arizona could seat more than 1200 people. For good visibility, the main floor slanted downward toward the altar. The floor was hardwood, and under each pew was a row of protruding iron vents, for heating and cooling.

One Sunday two six-year-old boys came to sit in church service for the first time in their lives. They sat at the rear of the church. For a while they were fascinated with the music, the announcements, the rituals. But midway through the sermon, Bobby got bored.

Inasmuch as it was marble season, Bobby had nearly thirty marbles stashed in his pockets. So now he decided to show a double handful of these to his friend.

And of course it was inevitable — a marble dropped onto the hardwood floor, and the law of gravity immediately went into operation.

When the first one dropped people all around were startled awake. In his haste to retrieve that one, Bobby dropped the whole double handful.

Down the floor they went, under the feet of the people, hitting the iron registers, *ping . . . plink . . . plink-plink . . . rattle . . . ping-rattle r-r-r-r-r-BANG* against the altar railing clear down at the front!

It was worse than a hailstorm. Nobody could hear the preacher — nobody was paying him any attention now anyway. Matters grew worse, because in their desperation the boys began to crawl under the long section of center pews, grabbing at marbles wherever they could, scraping worshipers' legs, and calling encouragement to one another.

Finally the good minister, smiling gently, helped the lads to their feet while the people stared.

"Your marbles," said he to the boys, "might be called 'holy rollers!' Just sit quietly down here now. I will be finished soon."

✝

*The wedding had been very impressive. Little Robin had sat through all of it, and now on arising to leave their pew she spoke loudly to her mother, "Why did the lady change her mind?"*

*Mother showed surprise. "Whatever do you mean, Robin dear?"*

*"Well, she walked down the aisle with one man, and walked back out with another."*

**26**

*Epistles? Of course you have heard what they are, or at least what the little girl in Sunday school said they are. Replied she when asked, "I guess they are the wives of the Apostles."*

✛

Mr. Wilson, a good churchman, was bald except for the fringes around his ears. In his pew one Sabbath, he kept scratching in the hair just over his right ear. On and on he scratched.

Finally, the small boy right behind him leaned over and stage-whispered, "Say, mister, you'll never catch him there. Why don't you run him out in the open?"

✛

Mother came into Sonny Smith's room shortly before breakfast, turned to Sonny and demanded, "Who didn't hang up his clothes before he went to bed?"

The lad gave prompt and perfect answer: "Adam."

✛

*The minister was rhapsodizing about the landscape of Canaan. "Just think of it!" he beamed at the class of youngsters. "A land flowing with milk and honey! I wonder what that would be like?"*

*Scratch Harris answered: "Sticky!"*

✛

Johnny was a public hero. "Now tell us, John," the teacher asked in Sunday school, "why did you so fearlessly rush out onto that thin lake ice to rescue your friend Joe?"

Replied Johnny, "Had to. He was wearing my skates."

"What reward does your mother give you?" asked the preacher of nine-year-old Randy, "when you have been a good boy all week?"

Said Randy, "She lets me stay home from church."

✠

"Boys, boys!" exclaimed mother, rushing to separate her fighting small sons. "Have you not heard of the Golden Rule?"

"Yeah," sniffled one, "But he did unto me first."

✠

*Pastor Ehrhardt of our church had been paying five-year-old Tommy Hale ten cents a week to keep his elderly grandfather awake during the sermon. One Sunday Tommy didn't deliver, and in the social hour after service Dr. Ehrhardt reminded him. "I know, sir," explained the lad, "but Grandfather pays me 15 cents to let him sleep."*

✠

"Why do we always say 'Amen' after each song?" a small lad asked his father.

"That means the song is over, son."

"Yes, but why don't we say 'Awomen?'"

"Son, maybe it's because all the songs we sing in church are *hymns!*"

✠

I resent what our new, young Director of Religious Education told my little girl recently. She asked him why we never see pictures of angels with whiskers such as her father often shows. "Because, dear," said he with a wink, "men who get to heaven make it only by a close shave."

Early one Saturday morning — too early — little Missy rushed into her parents' bedroom yelping, "Mommy, Mommy, what day is this?"

Mother aroused herself enough to say, "Saturday."

"Hurray!" cried Missy. "No school today! I have been praying for Saturday to come, and finally my prayers have been answered!"

✠

*Very young and earnest Harold Hathaway was kneeling beside his bed. "Dear God," prayed he, "if you can find some way to put the vitamins in candy and ice cream instead of in spinach and cod liver oil, I would sure appreciate it. Amen."*

✠

"God bless Mommy and Daddy," prayed the kindergartner, "and the man who fixes our TV."

✠

"Say your prayers," Mother commanded the child who was in bed with a slight fever, "and ask God to make you well."

"Why?" the child demanded, "isn't that what we are paying Dr. Monroe for?"

✠

Mary Lou had been naughty all morning. Finally in desperation her mother took action. "Go to your room," she ordered. "Stay there and think about how naughty you have been, and pray about it."

After a while Mary Lou returned to the kitchen and reported. "I thought about it and I prayed about it."

"Well," Mother ruled, "that ought to help to make

you be good."

"Oh, I doubt it," Mary Lou admitted, loftily. "You see, I didn't pray for God to make me good. I prayed for Him to help you to put up with me."

✠

Little Raymond was all aglow when he came home from Sunday school. "Teacher said something mighty nice about me when she prayed this morning," he reported.

"She did?" Father was interested. "What'd she say?"

"She said, 'We thank thee, dear God, for our food and Raymond.'"

✠

*His father had just taken five-year-old Ricky to see his first big college football game, and the lad came home thoroughly indoctrinated with collegiate methods. At dinner, Mother asked Ricky if he would offer the prayer and he readily agreed. He then bowed his head and said, "Thanks for this food, and bless us here at the table. Rah, rah, rah, dear Lord, give us more when you are able."*

✠

Fiduciary bargainings with the Lord are questionable at best, but probably He will forgive six-year-old Charlie Bill. The lad's father happened to overhear his bedtime prayer: "And God, if you will keep that Susie Smith from trying to kiss me, and will let me walk on my hands when she is looking, I will give you some money."

# 4.
# Marriage Miniatures

"So you and Jasper are married!" said the benevolent preacher to his church secretary. "And all along I thought it was just another flirtation."

Said she, "So did Jasper."

✠

*The preacher asked pretty Angela Auerglas, "When are you thinking of getting married?"*

*Said Angela, "Constantly."*

✠

"Beware," warned the preacher counseling a young man. "Many a time puppy love has led a man into a dog's life."

✠

The normally hale and hearty young bachelor was looking very woebegone and sad, so his pastor called on him, hoping to give aid and comfort. The young man managed finally to explain.

"I fell in love with the most beautiful girl in the world, pastor, but when I asked her to marry me, she refused."

"Now, now, my boy, don't take it to heart so. Any girl's 'no' quite frequently turns out to mean 'yes.'"

"Maybe so, sir. But this girl didn't say 'no'. She said, 'Oh phooey!'"

✠

*A tightwad entered a gift shop looking for a cheap*

*gift to send to a girl about to be married. Finally he found a glass vase that had been broken, and the clerk said he could have it for a quarter. He was delighted. He ordered it sent to the girl, figuring that she would think it had been broken in transit.*

*A month later he got a thank-you note: "I truly appreciate the vase, and it was so thoughtful of you to wrap each piece separately!"*

✠

The preacher's wife spoke to her man. "Do you think you may marry that Ellen Harris and Tom Baxter soon?"

"Well, I believe their engagement is a deep secret."

"Yes, so everybody is saying."

✠

"Whom did you marry?" they asked Sam.

"Experience," said he.

You understand, experience is the name men give to their mistakes.

✠

One young couple rushed into a minister's house demanding to be married immediately. "Here's the license. Use the short service; your wife and mother can be witnesses. Make it snappy," said the breathless groom.

The preacher obliged by marrying them, but he then admonished: "Marriage in haste is dangerous. What is your hurry?"

The young man had his bride already through

the door, but he called over his shoulder, "We're double parked."

✠

At another church the parson agreed to marry a young couple immediately after service one Sunday morning. Appropriately, he preached on the joys of family life, and then after the closing prayer he smiled benignly and said, "Now will those who wish to be married please come forward." Fifteen women and one man walked up the aisle!

✠

*One preacher was known to be an ardent fisherman, but he also was forgetful. He asked the groom, "Do you promise to love, honor and obey this woman?"*

*"I do," the groom replied, meekly.*

*"Okay," said the preacher turning to the bride. "Reel him in."*

✠

A rural groom, wearing a week's growth of beard and needing a hair cut, went to town and into a store. There he happened to pick up a hand mirror and look into it.

"I'll be switched," he muttered, "if here ain't a picture of my old pappy what died ten years ago."

He bought the mirror, to take home to his bride, telling her with pride how he had found his pappy's picture.

She opened the package, studied the mirror a moment, then snarled at her man: "This here ain't your pappy, this is a pitcher of one of them low-down, good-for-nothing gals you used to visit."

This led to a bitter quarrel, until the preacher happened along. So they asked *him* to decide whose portrait it was.

The preacher took the mirror, studied it, then ruled, "It ain't neither yore pappy nor any woman you ran around with. This here is a portrait of my uncle Ben who was hanged for stealin' horses."

✛

*"Statistics show that July is the most dangerous month for bridegrooms," the preacher told his flock of "young marrieds." "By then the June brides have progressed to the pie sections of their cookbooks."*

✛

The young daughter in one family was reaching out for Biblical information. "Daddy," she began, "why was Adam made before Eve?"

Daddy glanced around to be sure mother was out of hearing, then answered: "So that he would have a chance to say a few words, my dear."

✛

*A preacher was being kind. "George, my friend, you aren't looking well. Is something disturbing your soul?"*

*"I got troubles in my family life, rev-rend," said George.*

*"Oh dear. But you have always told people that your wife is a pearl."*

*"Yes, she is," said quick-witted George. "It's the mother-of-pearl who's making all the trouble."*

Two families had gathered in the minister's study to discuss a forthcoming wedding.

"The bride always wears white," said the preacher, "because a wedding is the happiest, most promising day of her life. White is the symbol of joy."

A cynical bachelor uncle spoke up. "Is that why the groom always wears black?"

✠

The shy young man contemplating marriage, asked his pastor, "If I do think of getting married, how much will the license cost me?"

The preacher, a little fed up that day anyhow, let him have it: "Five dollars down and your salary for the rest of your life."

✠

"Well, Henry," the pastor greeted a bridegroom heartily, "I am told that you signed up as skipper on the Good Ship Matrimony. Right?"

"No, sir," replied Henry. "My wife is the skipper, because I married a widow. I'm her second mate."

✠

*At one wedding reception, a certain young man stood in a corner looking gloomy. Thinking to cheer him, the pastor asked, "Well, have you kissed the bride?"*

*Said the gloomy young man, "Not lately."*

✠

"So you want a wife to share your life, son," remarked the elderly minister to the young man. "Well, just remember that a lot of shareholders end up as directors."

✝

Then, there is the case of poor Jasper Jukes. The wedding was under way, the bride was big and beaming, but the groom was meager and meek.

"Do you, Jasper, take this woman for better or for worse?" asked the preacher.

"I takes nothing," mumbled Jasper. "I is being took."

✝

"I spent so much time courting her," the young bridegroom told his minister, "that I finally had to marry her for my money."

✝

"What are your prospects, young man?" the girl's father demanded of the prospective groom.

"Pretty good, sir, unless your daughter has misled me."

✝

*Pete, walking up the avenue with his friend said, "I hear Cupid almost got you last month."*

*"Yep," admitted the friend. "I had an arrow escape."*

✝

One Sunday in June the dour-faced minister stood up, walked to his pulpit and said, "First, an announcement: All of you who plan to be married this month, please come forward during the singing of the opening hymn."

The opening hymn: "Rescue the Perishing."

"Oh, pastor," cried the bride-to-be, "I have just learned that I am engaged to a man who cannot bear children."

"Well," replied her pastor, "you shouldn't expect *too* much of a fellow."

✝

Tip to all newlyweds: they will be very happy if he will listen to her describe in detail how a friend's dress was made, and if she will listen to him describe in detail how a football game was played.

✝

*In Doldrum Theological Seminary, Dr. Saddlie Thredbaire said to his class in English literature, "Tell me the two most important facts about Milton."*

*One young man gave serious thought to the matter, then said, "Well sir, he got married and wrote* Paradise Lost. *Then his wife died, and he wrote* Paradise Regained."

✝

Milo Milquetoast was so henpecked that he finally moved out to the woodshed to get away from his wife's nagging. He lived out there for months, and they spoke very little to each other, though occasionally she would bring him a pie or a cake.

The preacher came to talk to Milo about it, but couldn't see any way to solve their problem. "You say that she is terrible?" the parson asked. "You say she is absolutely intolerable?"

"No," admitted Milo, "I wouldn't go that far. You know, she *does* make a good neighbor."

In case you men haven't heard — a bridegroom is a man who has just lost his self-control.

✛

*Sandy McTaggart, the well known Scot, was about to be married, so somewhat anxiously he approached his best man.*

*"Do ye suppose, Dougal, they'll be after throwing old shoes at Rachel and me when we leave the church?"*

*"I ha' no doot they weel do so. 'Tis the custom."*

*"Weel, please, good friend, could you just mention around among the people that Rachel wears size five, and I wear 'elevens?' "*

✛

Then there was poor Alex the Scot who was in a dither of emotion. He was in love with pretty Jean in the next village, yet lacked the nerve to tell her so. Finally one Tuesday morning, at 9:30, the Presbyterian pastor prevailed upon him to telegraph Jean a proposal of marriage.

At 8 P.M. Alex rushed to the pastor's house on his very special Cloud 9, shouting, "She has accepted me; her answer just came in. You weel marry us soon, pastor?"

The minister was not excited. He scowled, saying, "I dunno that you should marry the girl after all. Should you really marry one who would wait all day to give you her answer?"

"Oh, aye, aye, aye, pastor!" exulted Alex. "Any lassie who weel wait for the cheaper rates at night is the wife for me!"

"A modest girl never pursues a man," the pastor counseled his college co-ed class at Sunday school, "any more than a mouse trap pursues a mouse."

✠

"The Hollywood version of the famous quotation," said the Rev. Bill Eckels, "seems to be, 'Thou shalt love one, another, and another.'"

✠

*Two brides were talking, giggling, swapping experiences. "Was Bill excited at your wedding?" Harriet asked.*

*"I'll say he was!" replied pretty Nancy Fern. "He kissed the minister and gave me ten dollars."*

✠

You know how it is at a big party, where everybody is jammed into one room and everyone is talking. Wry Rev. Tom Fitch of Chicago — a bachelor — attended a wedding reception like that. As he moved past the receiving line, with a din of voices dominating the hall, he murmured to each of the kin and in-laws of the bride, "My grandmother just threw herself off a high cliff and was killed."

Endless smiles and words of acknowledgment proved that nobody was really listening. "Thank you very much!" . . . "Oh how nice!" . . . "Yes indeed, wasn't it!" . . . "How wonderful of you to say so!" . . . "So happy you could see it" . . . That sort of thing.

Then he came to the bridegroom himself, who, in a lather of excitement anyway, shouted back at his pastor friend, "Great, great, Tom, and it's about time you took the same step! Let me know when you do, so I can celebrate!"

Man: "You ought to see the beautiful altar at our church."

Girl: "Okay, lead me to it."

✠

"Father," asked the preacher's small son, "what makes a man always give a woman a diamond ring when he aims to marry her?"

Replied his father: "The woman."

✠

*The honest preacher was trying to help a prospective groom buy an engagement ring, and he said, "It might be just as well if you bought the special, three-piece combination."*

*"What's that?" asked the young man, surprised.*

*"Engagement, wedding, and teething."*

✠

John and Mary were very much in love, and John finally summoned the courage to propose. But he was honest, so he said, "There is one thing. I love you all right, but I think you ought to know that I am a somnambulist."

"I don't care," said Mary. "We can go to your church one Sunday, and mine the next."

✠

The church newsletter to parishioners, reporting on the wedding of the pretty choir member, contained a typographical error or two:

"The bride was beautifully retired in white, but the bridesmaids all wore punk gowns. All the flowers and decorations also were punk."

# 5.
# Missionary Madness

The missionary from a Boston church called on an Indian family in Oklahoma. Being a very gracious man, he inquired, "Do you speak any foreign language?"

"Yes," replied the Cherokee smartly. "English."

✠

*"I come from New York," said the tourist in Salt Lake City to a local girl. "I imagine you don't even know where New York is."*

*"Yes, I do," she assured him quickly. "Our Mormon church has a missionary there."*

✠

The somewhat crusty old missionary had been called back to the States for a visit, and was now getting tired of the endless round of dinners, parties and teas in his honor. At one of the latter, the gushy women were pestering him for "stories of your adventures in the South Sea Islands."

Recklessly he told them, "Well, yes, once I discovered a whole tribe of women, very wild women, who had no tongues."

"No tongues!" cried Madam Chairman. "Heavens, how could they talk?"

"They couldn't," said he grimly. "*That's* what made them wild."

The back country missionary had walked many miles alone. Finally he put up for the night in an isolated farm home. The family was honored to have him, but shortly before dawn the daughter of the house came into his room, shook him awake and said, "Please to git up, sir. Ma, she wants the sheet for a table cloth."

✛

The tough and stolid Indians of America finally realized the proper way to do things, so in spite of free handouts from the white government over the past century, they went on strike. Food, housing, raiment, horses, cars and such weren't enough they said, they demanded the fringe luxuries such as refrigerators, radios and color TV sets. Their spokesman, a very stern-faced "savage," was adamant about it, saying little, but making it clear that the redskins' demands must be met. Government agents were at wit's end.

So a missionary preacher was called in as intermediary. But all he could get from the red spokesman was "Ugh, ugh," and concluded that the man spoke little English. He worked hard with the government agents, and won some concessions.

Then he strained to tell the red man: "The government will increase your allowances one dollar a week, and I recommend that you take it. Do you understand me, do you understand my words?"

The stolid Indian looked hard at the paleface preacher and said, "Well, ugh, yes, I shall recommend that my people accept the offer, provided the bureaucratic hierarchy in Washington is willing to make it retroactive. Would the agents be amenable to that?"

*The missionary minister allegedly rode up to the backwoods town, and a committee met him with this question: "What'll you charge for a sermon Sunday?"*

*"Thirty dollars."*

*"We ain't got that much."*

*"Fifteen dollars, then."*

*"We ain't got that much, either."*

*"How much have you got?"*

*The committeemen looked embarrassed, then one asked, "Ain't you got a sermon you could give us for about five dollars?"*

*"Yes, I have," the preacher nodded. "But I have to warn you — it ain't worth a hoot."*

✠

The home missionary also has his troubles. This one was medically trained, so when he called at the farm home of Sebe Cornstalk, he read the assembled family a chapter of the Bible, then probed into the delicate matter of cleanliness.

"Mr. Cornstalk, may I recommend that you purchase a bathtub for your large family. They — uh — appear to need one."

"Nawp, won't do it, parson," replied Sebe. "Had one once, and it killed grandpappy."

"A bathtub killed your grandfather? How in the world could that happen?"

"Well preacher, it was a fine, pretty tub, so we put it on the front porch there, filled it with water, and all of us started taking baths. First, Mama bathed. Then big daughter bathed, then second daughter, then oldest son, then middle son, then Grandma, then the twins, then Uncle Giveahoot, then me."

"Yes?" the missionary preacher encouraged.

"Well, finally it came Grandpappy's turn, and him being last is what killed him. He got in that there tub and died in the quicksand."

✠

A foreign missionary came back to visit his home church in Kansas. He showed movies of kangaroos hopping about the wilderness, and said, "These are native to Australia."

"Oh, dear," exclaimed one lady in the congregation misunderstanding, "and to think my Cousin Emma married one of them!"

✠

*The good missionary in Southeast Asia tried to double as Army chaplain whenever needed. One day he approached a black soldier and gently asked, "My good man, are you Indo-Chinese?"*

*The man grinned big and replied, "No, suh, Ah is outdo'-Mississippi."*

✠

Another American missionary had visited Vietnam before the war there. One day he saw a well-dressed Vietnamese gentleman riding a horse, and about 30 feet behind him walked the wife. The missionary stopped the man to inquire about that, and was told that it was the custom.

Duties took the missionary home, but two years passed and he returned to Vietnam, when the war had become a horror. Suddenly, he saw the same Vietnamese gentleman riding along on a horse. But this time, the wife was walking about 30 feet in *front* of him.

He stopped the rider and said, "Two years ago your wife was walking behind you, and you said it was the Vietnamese custom. Now she is walking out in front. How come the change?"

Replied the Vietnamese gentleman briefly, "Land mines."

✠

The most fascinating of all missionary outposts — at least to us who remain at home — are those storied islands where cannibals live. And indeed, many are the stories that emanate from there, (all true, of course).

For instance, the new missionary arrived, met the big, fat black cannibal chief and asked him, "Whatever became of my predecessor here?"

"Oh," explained the suave chief, "he made a trip into the interior."

✠

The cannibal cook had a big fire going under his pot, and asked his king, "Shall I boil this Catholic missionary, Chief?"

"Don't be stupid," growled His Majesty. "This one is a friar."

✠

*History records the following concerning beloved Queen Liliuokalani of the Hawaiian Islands. A newspaper reporter was once interviewing her, and she told him that she had British blood in her veins.*

*"How did that ever happen?" he asked the dark skinned queen.*

*"Well," replied Her Majesty, "Captain Cook and a lot of English missionaries came over here, and my ancestors ate them."*

The Baptist missionary said to the cannibal chief, "Do your people know anything about our religion, sir?"

Replied His Majesty, "Well, we did get a little taste of it when your last missionary was here."

✠

A very young Catholic priest was sent to the cannibal islands, to help an elderly priest who was about to retire. The new man asked, "Well, Father, how have you gotten along with these man-eaters?"

"I have made *some* progress," the old priest replied. "On Fridays now, they eat only fishermen."

✠

*The cannibal islands had been visited by modern-day English missionaries with modern equipment, but they didn't get to stay long. Later, however, the black chieftain went to London, and of course was called to visit Her Majesty, the Queen.*

*"Did you have a pleasant trip?" she asked.*

*"Screech, hon-nk, skritch-skritch, whistle, zizz-z-z-z," said the cannibal king, then added in perfect English, "Yes, thank you, Your Majesty."*

*She politely ignored the oddity, and asked, "And are your people happy?"*

*"Ziz-z-z-z, honk, screech, skritch-skritch, whistle, ras-s-sp," said the chief. "Yes, Your Most Gracious Majesty, they seem to be quite content. And I trust your subjects are happy also."*

*"They are fine, thank you. But do tell me — where did you learn to speak such perfect English?"*

*Replied the cannibal island king: "Honk, skritch-scratch, zip-zip-zip, ft-ft-ft, scree-e-e-eeech, whistle, er-r-r-r. I learned by short-wave radio."*

# 6.
# Pedigreed Pastors

Mrs. Weems, a worrier, went to her pastor and said, "Oh, Dr. Boice, whatever shall I do? My husband Milton seems to be wandering in his mind."

"Now, now," the pastor soothed, "don't be too disturbed. I know Milton, and I'm sure he can't go very far."

✝

"I *can't* go around practicing what I
preach," says good friend Ernest Douglas.
"I'd work myself to death."

✝

*"Opportunity knocks only once,"* one preacher
*warned his flock, "but temptation bangs on your
door for years."*

✝

Possibly the best loved of the malapropisms is that of the pompous senior preacher of a fashionable church who was reprimanding his young assistant. Growled he, "Why did you not deliver that message exactly as I gave it to you?"

The contrite young man said, "I did the best I could, sir."

"The best you could indeed! If I had known I was going to send a donkey, I would have gone myself!"

✝

The inevitable smart aleck who haunts every church patio during coffee hour after services approached the pastor there one Sunday and asked the Rev. Aaron Powers, "What clerical advice have you for drivers who drink?"

Replied the preacher, "Jug not that ye be not jugged."

✛

*Consider, the minister who, in soliciting funds for his church, was turned down by a curt letter which said:*

> *"As far as I can see, this Christian business*
> *is one continuous give, give, give."*

*The good pastor wrote back: Thank you for the best definition of the Christian life I have ever read."*

✛

Truly, a preacher sometimes gets a chance to revenge himself on his flock. One week the secretary to the Rev. Aaron Powers asked Huck Johnson to be a greeter at the church door on Sunday morning. Huck's wife pressured him into accepting, even though Huck hadn't been to church for nearly two years.

Now Huck was a friendly extrovert, and rather enjoyed himself shaking hands and greeting the worshipers. Everything went along fine at first. Then a late comer entered the door. Huck thought he looked familiar, but couldn't quite place him. So he smiled, stuck out his hand and said, "Good morning. Mighty glad to see you here today."

The rather serious man replied, "Oh, I try to get here as often as I can," then bowed, strode on down the aisle to the pulpit and started the morning service.

*Another preacher absentmindedly left his sermon manuscript on the pulpit one Sunday, and the sexton, cleaning up, found it next morning. The sexton read it.*

*Down the wide margin, the preacher had red-penciled reminders for himself, such as, "Lower voice here" . . . "Pause here". . . . "Wipe brow here." . . . "Look upward here." . . . "Speak softly here."*

*On page six was a long passage of text, and beside it the pastor had written, "Argument weak here,* yell!

✠

Said the highly popular, highly successful pastor of the First Presbyterian Church in Phoenix, "Humor is to life what shock absorbers are to automobiles."

✠

"It's just as well to forget your *old* troubles," the pastor said to me one night, after he had tired of hearing me whine. "Because a lot of interesting new ones will soon be coming along."

✠

One congregation had called a new preacher, and was giving a reception in his honor. All the church folk were there, including the retiring minister, who had not yet met his successor. But the new one came along the receiving line and was introduced.

"Ah, so happy to meet you, sir," said the new man. "And is this your most charming wife?"

The old preacher, disgruntled anyway, let him have it. "This is my *only* wife."

The handsome, new young minister had agreed to address the coeds at a local Junior College, so in anticipation they quickly put out flowers, then varnished all the chairs. Unfortunately they had a muggy spell of weather, and the varnish didn't dry well. So when the preacher was introduced, he couldn't rise from his chair without much pulling, much ado.

At last he got to the rostrum and said to the girls, "I had expected to bring you a plain and unvarnished tale, but circumstances make it impossible."

✝

*Not all preachers are quick on the uptake. Vain Mrs. Melissa Mayfield was gushing along as usual at the church tea, when she said, "Oh, dear, I just hate to think of my twenty-sixth birthday!"*

*"Why?" asked Dr. Obtuse. "What went wrong?"*

✝

"Some ladies who never talk much," avowed the pastor after a session with the Women's Missionary League, "just never had an operation."

✝

*The much-too-dignified young bachelor minister pulled away from the much-too-ardent choir soprano saying, "Please, Miss Smith, you are steaming my glasses!"*

✝

The preacher believed in youth work, so one week he printed this notice — typographical error included — in his mimeographed parish newsletter: "High school girls who are interested in homes they expect

**50**

to ruin in the future, are invited to a seminar at the church on Friday evening at eight."

✠

*Women dearly love to call at the pastor's study. One of them stayed overly long with poor Dr. Patience, but finally she said, "I must be going, I really must go, pastor. Do you know — when I came in here I had a headache, and now it is lost entirely."*

*"No it isn't," declared he, softly. "I have it."*

✠

Another lady bore had been in the preacher's study for more than an hour. She was running on and on, saying, "Speaking of accidents, reminds me of the time —"

Instantly the minister leaped in. "My goodness, you are so right, madam! I had no *idea* it was this late! Goodbye!"

✠

"Americans are worshiping in the cult of the immaterial," Pastor Bill Vogel told his flock in one of his cuter moments. "Women's styles today command less cloth, less criticism, more money and more attention than ever before."

✠

"What man would be without woman,"
said the saintly S. Omar Barker of New
Mexico, "is certainly not apparent."

✠

Somebody asked the Rev. Roy Shepler what he and his family did for vacations. Said he, "We go away every third year."

"Every third? But what do you do for the other two years?"

"Well, for the first one we talk about last year's trip. For the second year we talk about next year's trip."

✝

His distinguished and very conceited eminence the new pastor was telling out-of-town colleagues about the first Sunday morning at his new pastorate. "I simply had the congregation glued to their seats," declared he, loftily.

"Marvelous," another preacher murmured. "Clever of you to think of it."

✝

*Bartholomew Gotrocks was trying to impress the calling minister with his wealth, and showed him all the luxurious details of his country estate. "I had all these trees moved right here to my lawn," he boasted. "Had them set up in perfect geometrical pattern this way."*

*"My, my," murmured the pastor, "it just goes to show you what wonders God could perform if only He had money!"*

✝

Fisherman Bill Norman was bragging to his pastor, "Wow, did I ever catch a trout! It was huge! Colossal!" Bill spread his hands wide. It must have weighed 30 pounds. I never *saw* such a fish!"

Pastor Bill Vogel remained calm, saying, "I believe you."

A new pastor came to the small town, studied the church records, then walked to the office of the local weekly newspaper. "Sir," said he to the editor, "I find that you have 61 subscribers in my congregation. Wouldn't that merit a little church news each week?"

"Sure. Just sit down there and write your notice, Reverend."

So the preacher wrote: "The First Baptist Church of Crudneyville Township has a new pastor, who cordially invites everyone to come and hear him next Sunday at 11 o'clock. In the promulgation of Christianity, three books are necessary, and the church has one of them. Please bring the other two. The three are: the Bible, the hymnbook, and the checkbook."

✛

*The parish pest, a young and vain member who had too-long hair and a too-short bank account, said fatuously to the preacher, "Pastor, would you advise me to marry a beautiful girl, or a sensible girl?"*

*The good minister had already been through too much with this man, so he let him have both barrels. "I fear you will never be able to marry either kind."*

*"But pastor, why not?" He was indignant.*

*"Well, any beautiful girl* could *do better, and any sensible girl* would *do better."*

✛

A preacher, deep in thought, was ambling across a busy street and almost got hit. The motorist screeched to a stop, looked out and shouted, "You pedestrians walk as if you owned the streets!"

Unperturbed, the preacher replied, "Yes, and many of you motorists drive as if you owned your cars."

**53**

"We have to remedy the status quo," the pastor told his flock.

"What's that mean?" one none too literate brother demanded.

"Status quo is Latin for the mess we is in."

✠

The very illiterate and very RFD church session was in a business meeting. An item was introduced by Elder Hiram Phudge: "Our church sholy does need a cuspidor."

The somewhat dense pastor nodded approval, "Ve'y well, I hereby appoints Brother Sam Johnson as church cuspidor. Nex' item?"

✠

*This was night service, and a guest pastor had arrived. In due time he stood up, smiled widely and said, "Ladies and gents, if I had et a gallon of dried applies' then had swallered a gallon of water before I left home, I couldn't be more swelled up than I is right now over the big crowd of you what has turned out to hear me this evenin'."*

✠

Another guest minister whipped up his horse and galloped up to the First Backwoods Church just in time for the morning service. The congregation was patiently waiting for him. So he entered the pulpit and right off said, "Now sisteren and bretheren, I has a five-dollar sermon, and a one-dollar sermon, and a ten-dollar sermon. So we will begin by taking up the collection, then I'll know what kind of sermon you all wants."

One 80-year-old preacher had to have an operation, a very serious one. He fought the idea, but had the operation, and afterward fought to live. He did manage to recover, then his doctor ragged him: "You know, preacher, for a man who is constantly talking about the glories of heaven, you sure put up a terrific battle to avoid going there."

✟

*Then, there is the unquestionably true story of the tough old hill country preacher who just didn't like any kind of music, and figured that surely the very thought of it was the devil's own invention.*

*"How can you possibly say that, pastor?" a new young choir director asked him when visiting his church. "Music is the language of the soul, expressing the inexpressible."*

*"Don't keer if it unscrews the inscrutable," said the tough old preacher, "I'm ag'in it!"*

✟

A Tired Minister's Farewell:

"Brothers and Sisters, I must say goodbye. I don't think God loves this church, because none of you has ever died. I don't think you love each other, because I never have married any of you. I don't think you love me, because you have not paid my salary. Your donations are moldy fruit and wormy apples, and 'by their fruits ye shall know them.' Brethren, I am going to a better place. I have been called to be chaplain at the State Penitentiary. Where I go you can not come yet, but I go to prepare a place for you. And may the good Lord have mercy on your souls."

A reformer is somebody who wants *his* conscience to be *your* guide.

✜

A pastor was riding on one of those slow, milk-stop trains that seemed never to get anywhere, and he was reading his Bible. The conductor came along, smiled, and asked, "Do you see anything about the railroad in that Book?"

"Yes," the parson assured him. "In the very first chapter it says that the Lord made every creeping thing."

✜

*"If you do not feel as close to God as you once did," warned the pastor, "make no mistake about which one of you has moved."*

✜

"In designing man's hinges," says the Rev. Tom Barker, "the Creator knew he would have little occasion to pat himself on the back."

✜

One pastor in a fashionable church at least broke through the crust of self-satisfaction and pseudo-sophistication that had marked the pompous congregation. He was talking about agnostics.

"Some of you people say, 'I don't believe or disbelieve.'" Here the minister leaned over his pulpit and almost shouted in exasperation: "Why, you could sit on *that* egg for the rest of your life, and you wouldn't hatch a thing!"

# 7.
# Parishable Prayers

"The trouble with too many prayers," suggested the Rev. Donald Hall to his congregation, "is that they are addressed not to God, but to the government."

✠

*The Rev. Mebane Ramsay, First Presbyterian pastor at Hagerman, New Mexico, reports that his mind and tongue got twisted while leading "The Lord's Prayer" one Sunday, and the petition came out — "Lead us not into temptation, but deliver us from righteousness."*

*After the service, his congregation assured him that the prayer would be easily answered.*

✠

Good Father Paul Hogarty told his congregation one Sunday that it was almost impossible not to be distracted while saying prayers. The next day he met parishioner Geoff Geoffroy on the street.

"Father," Geoff began, "I think you were wrong about that distraction business. Now I ride horseback a lot, and I often pray as I ride. Nothing, absolutely nothing distracts me."

Father Paul smiled gently, then said, "Very well. I know where I can get a fine new Arabian stallion free. I will give him to you, Geoff, if you can say just one 'Our Father' right now, without distraction."

Geoff grinned, bowed his head and started in: " 'Our Father who art in heaven, hallowed be thy name. . .' say, Father, do I get a saddle with the horse, too?"

✝

The clothing store manager was reprimanding a meek clerk. "See here, Weems, I understand you have been trying to go over my head."

"Oh, no, sir," poor Weems trembled. "How ever could you have heard that?"

"Isn't it true that you have been praying for a raise in pay?"

✝

*Miserly old Giveahoot Hoskins, known to be a multi-millionaire skinflint, was very sick in the hospital, but the preacher dutifully called on him.*

*"Pray for me," gasped Uncle Giveahoot, eyes rolling toward heaven, "and if I get well I will give the church $50,000."*

*Of course the good pastor prayed, and sure enough, the old miser got well. A month later the pastor tactfully reminded him that he had promised to give the church $50,000 if he recovered.*

*"I did that?" he exclaimed, appalled. "Just goes to show you how sick I really was, parson. Good day."*

✝

Sometimes it's a simple case of stage fright. When there was no musical instrument for a certain prayer meeting one night, the pastor asked a good layman to start singing:

> *I must needs go home*
> *by the way of the cross*

The man croaked twice, "I must needs go home," and each time, he froze up in self-consciousness. Finally the pastor intervened. "Observing our brother's propensity, let us pray."

✠

An Episcopalian preacher was invited to give a sermon in a tiny suburban Baptist church whose members took a dim view of his views anyway. The time came to take up the collection, and the Episcopalian gave his hat to a man to pass. Presently the hat was returned to him — and not a single coin had been put in.

The preacher lifted his eyes to heaven and prayed anyhow: "I thank thee, O Lord, that I have got my hat back from this congregation."

✠

It is recorded that the elderly Dr. Wordsmith was a guest at a meeting conducted by the famous Dwight L. Moody, who asked his guest to offer the prayer. Dr. Wordsmith began slowly and softly, rose to a crescendo, finally got completely bogged down in the overflow of his own verbosity, praying on, and on, and on.

After a long interval, Mr. Moody spoke up and said, "While our brother is finishing his prayer, we will sing Hymn No. 71."

✠

"O Lord," prayed the patriotic Texas preacher, "we pause to thank You for the many blessings brought to our state, and we beseech You to look with compassion on those many places where Your feet have not trod."

The 22-year-old minister and the 72-year-old bishop happened to be traveling together. They shared a hotel bedroom their first night out, and at bedtime both knelt for their devotions. The older man prayed very briefly.

The young man stayed on his knees for 20 minutes, then crawled under the covers and said to his boss, "You didn't pray very long, sir."

"No," replied the bishop. "I keep prayed up."

✜

A hypocrite, we are told, is a man who writes a book praising atheism, then prays that it will sell.

✜

The good Presbyterian pastor in Glasgow was walking down the street when two bairns thought to nag him. "Reverent," one lad grinned, "have ye heard th' news. The devil is dead!" Both boys nodded that it was so.

But they had met their match. "In that case," said the dominie, "I must hurry to church and pray for two fatherless bairns."

✜

The minister of the First Impecunious Rural Church was in fine form. "Does any of you folks want us to pray for yur shortcomings?" he asked, at one service when all pews were full.

A brother stood up. "I does, preacher."

"What is yo' problem, brother?"

"I is a spendthrift, suh. I makes big money, and I is reckless with the way I throws my money around."

"Lawd, lawd, that sholy *is* bad. Friends, let us

**60**

pray for our reckless brother — right after we takes up the collection."

✠

None-too-brilliant Jim Jukes came to the minister one Monday and said, "Parson, I want you to pray for me. The doctor says I have a floating kidney."

"But James, I don't know how to pray for physical things. I pray for spiritual betterment, so I wouldn't know how to pray for a floating kidney."

"Then parson, how come yesterday in church you prayed for all the loose livers?"

✠

For more than a year a little old charwoman who lived on the wrong side of the tracks had been trying to join a fashionable downtown church. The pastor was not eager to have a seedy looking person in faded, out-of-style clothes sitting in a pew next to his rich members. When she called for the fifth time to discuss membership, he put her off for the fifth time.

"I tell you what," said he unctuously, "you just go home tonight and have a talk with God about it. Later you can tell me what He said."

The poor woman went her way. Weeks moved into months, and the pastor saw no more of her, and his conscience did hurt a little. Then one day he encountered her scrubbing floors in an office building, and felt impelled to inquire. "Did you have your little talk with God, Mrs. Washington?" he asked.

"Oh, my, yes," she said, "I talked with God, as you said."

"Ah, and what answer did He give you?"

"Well parson," she pushed back a wisp of stringy

hair with a sudsy hand, "God said for me not to get discouraged, but to keep trying. He said that He Himself had been trying to get into your church for 20 years, with no more success than I have had."

✠

An aged Negro philosopher once told his friends, "Unless a man is in trouble, his prayers ain't got no suction."

✠

One home had a new cook. When the maid had served the cook's first culinary offering, she was asked what the family thought about it.

"I'm not sure," said the maid. "They said nothing about your food, but they prayed before they ate."

✠

The nice old maid believed in prayer. One night in a fit of loneliness she knelt at her bedside and said, "Dear Lord, I ask nothing for myself, but please send my mother a fine, handsome son-in-law."

✠

The priest visited Pat in the hospital, saw him all bandaged around the head, and said, "Patrick, my son, I shall pray that you may forgive your Jewish friend Hymie for hitting you with that piece of iron pipe."

Patrick mumbled through his gauze, "Best ye just wait until I get well, Your Riv-rince. Then ye can pray for Hymie."

# 8.
# Unsaintly Saints

*It is regrettable that a man must do many fine things to prove that he is good, but only one evil thing to prove that he is bad.*

✠

A minister concluded a powerful sermon on the Ten Commandments. As the people filed out, glum-faced Oscar Quagmire was overheard to remark, "Well, anyway, I have never made a graven image."

✠

Saints and sinners are everywhere, of course, and sometimes it is hard to tell which is which. One of them turned up in the rural store operated by Old Man Sorghum, near the crossroads. He was running for sheriff, so he made a little speech to "the boys" gathered there.

"I can tell you men," said he, "that I know what the seven deadly sins is, and I can further tell you that I ain't never committed one of them." He nodded his head knowingly.

But Old Man Sorghum spoke up: "Which one, mister?"

✠

The Rev. Horace Checkup, a conscientious preacher, faced Deacon Schmieder and said, "Deacon, I am told that you went to the baseball game instead of to church last Sunday."

"That's a lie!" snapped the Deacon, "and I've got the fish to prove it!"

Dialing in a hurry, people sometimes do get wrong phone numbers. One day a pastor was studying the Bible in his office when his telephone rang. He heard the voice of one of his deacons say, "Hello, Sam? Say, Sam, send me over two quarts of Scotch, and a case of gin. I'm having a party tonight."

The minister was indignant. "Mr. Williams! I think you should know that this is not Sam's Liquor Store, and this is not Sam. This is the Rev. I. M. Ernest speaking!"

A short pause followed, then Mr. Williams spoke in surprise. "Dr. Ernest? Then what are *you* doing over at Sam's?"

✠

*At two o'clock in the morning a man telephoned Dr. Harry Emerson Fosdick: "Doc, I understand you are a very schmart man. So tell me, what is the differench between a fundamentalish and a modernish?"*

*Dr. Fosdick was kind. "My good man, it is very late. Come to my office later on and I will explain."*

*"No, no, Doc, that won't do. Later on I will be sober, and then it won't make no differench."*

✠

The good preacher was walking past a saloon. A man staggered out, exuding fumes of alcohol. The preacher touched his arm and spoke.

"Now, my good man, reflect. Soon you will die. If you arrive at the Pearly Gates and your breath is reeking with liquor, will St. Peter let you in?"

The inebriated one looked blearily back at him and said, "Preasher, when I go to heaven, I eshpect to leave my breath behind."

"The devil," says good preacher Bill Vogel, "is willing for a person to confess Christianity, so long as he does not practice it."

✠

"But parson," argued the honest car salesman in his parish, "you are minister of a big, fashionable church, so you *need* this prestige automobile. It will positively last you a lifetime. Besides that, you'll get more for it when you turn it in on next year's model."

✠

*Two businessmen were "friendly enemies." One ran for City Council. "I want you to vote for me, Horace," he said to his friend and enemy.*

*Horace grimaced. "If you were St. Peter himself I wouldn't vote for you."*

*Retorted the first man quickly, "If I were St. Peter, you wouldn't be in my district!"*

✠

Elderly Mrs. McTavish had an apple orchard. She was not only Scotch to the core, she was a perpetual complainer. Nothing was ever right on her farm. Even when the apple crop that year turned out to be the best ever, with large, luscious apples on every tree, and no disease or damage in them, just a perfect crop all the way, she was not happy. The preacher thought this a good time to point up the good bounty and cure her continual grumbling.

"How wonderful, Sister McTavish!" he exulted, viewing her orchard when he called. "I am so happy for you, and I know you are happy too over this fine crop of apples."

"Humph!" she growled. "They are all big ones. Where's the little ones and the rotten ones for the pigs?"

✠

One preacher happened to be interviewing a wealthy parishioner, who loved to talk about himself. "Why, do you know, pastor," said the rich one, "I came into this town barefooted and without a dime to my name, and just look at me now."

"I have always understood you were born here," said the minister.

"I was. And doesn't that prove what I just said?"

✠

Another preacher was interviewing a man noted for his shiftless ways. "Now Roscoe, my friend, how is it that you are always *looking* for a job, but never seem to *find* one?"

Big Roscoe grinned happily and replied, "Skill, reverend; skill."

✠

*Still another minister was walking down the street one day when a bum asked him for a dime. "Ah, my good man," replied the minister, "you are making the wrong approach to life. You need brains more than money."*

*The panhandler explained: "Sir, I just asked you for what I figured you had the most of."*

✠

Then there was the church missionary who went down to the slums to help his fellow man, and who met his own particular frustrations. He found a man leaning against a pole as if downcast, so he approached the fellow, placed a gentle hand on his shoulder, and said, "My friend, do you hear the constant ticking of that clock on yonder tower? Even if we don't actually hear it, we know it marches on, tick . . . tock . . . tick . . . tock. And oh, my dear brother, do you know what day that inexorable ticking of time brings closer and closer to us?"

The man nodded and said, "Sure. Payday."

✠

*Bernie Einstein weighed 248 pounds already, and did not always order strictly kosher meals. One morning at breakfast he decided that heaven would overlook the matter if he ate a bite or two of bacon, so he ordered bacon and enjoyed it, stifling his conscience all the while.*

*He had barely swallowed the last delicious morsel, paid his check and stepped outside onto the sidewalk, when lightning darted from the sky, struck a nearby light pole, and sent down a deluge of rain.*

*"My, my," grumbled Bernie, huddling under his coat and running toward the nearest temple, "all that fuss over just two little strips of bacon!"*

✠

The parishioner, of course, often gets the better of the dominie. One Friday Father O'Hara came to a lumbering camp, and caught big Mike Murphy eating sausage. "Mike!" he cried. "Meat on Friday?"

"These sausages ain't meat, Father."

"Of course they are. And for penance, you can just bring a truck load of wood to my home."

Mike bowed to the penance. He borrowed a truck, loaded it with sawdust, and soon was shoveling it

**67**

out at the priest's home. The man of God came onto him. "Mike, why are you putting that sawdust here?"

"This is your wood, Father."

"You are foolish, man. Sawdust isn't wood."

"Well, Father," said the unrepentant Mike, "if sawdust ain't wood, then them sausages wasn't meat."

✠

The sermon had been long and dry, and at the close of it the minister asked for a meeting of the church board. The first man to arrive at the meeting was a stranger.

"Evidently you misunderstood," the preacher told him. "I called for a meeting of the board."

"Yeah, I know," said the stranger, "and if anybody here was more bored than I was, I want to meet him."

✠

*"Half the people in church," said the chairman of the Board of Elders, "are willing to work, and the other half are willing to let them."*

✠

A philosopher and a preacher were talking. Said the preacher: "Yes, you philosophers are comparable to blind people in dark rooms looking for black cats that are not there."

"Possibly," the philosopher agreed. "But you preachers always find them."

✠

Then there were the three Scotsmen who were sitting together in church one Sunday morning when the pastor made a strong pitch for money to help a worthy cause. He said he wanted every person in the congregation to put two dollars in the offering. As the usher neared the Scotsmen's pew they came near to the point of panic, until sound financial inspiration suddenly struck them. One of them fainted, and the other two hastily carried him out.

✠

A millionaire soap manufacturer moved into the community, and the pastor thought it his duty to sound the man out about his immortal soul. He decided to begin gently, with a little ego sop. "To what," he asked the man, "do you owe your remarkable financial success?"

"Clean living, pastor," avowed the soap man, "clean living."

✠

*The renowned Bishop Kinsolving, in New York City, once asked a cab driver to take him to Christchurch. The cab driver took him to St. Mary's, instead.*

*"You misunderstood me," said the good bishop. "I asked for Christchurch."*

*"If He's in town, sir, this is where you'll find Him."*

✠

As a Presbyterian I had to face up to an embarrassing situation while visiting the Methodist church last Sunday. The collection plate came by, and I had nothing smaller than a dollar bill.

✠

The minister of the backwoods Baptist church was in fine form. "All who wants their souls washed white as snow, stand up," he demanded.

Only one man remained seated, so of course the pastor inquired, "How come you don't want your soul washed, Brother Jones?"

"I already had it washed."

"Where at?"

"Over at the Presbyterian church," said the visitor.

"You stand up, suh. You ain't had yo' soul washed, you has had it dry cleaned!"

✠

Good Father Paul Hogarty got into that unconscionable traffic jam that only Los Angeles develops. He took a wrong direction on a one-way street, got turned around, ran a red light, struck a sign pole, and finally parked beside a fire hydrant. An Irish Catholic cop came up, saluted and said, "Best move along now, Father. But I have to warn you, sor. The policeman on the *next* corner is a Baptist."

✠

*A revival meeting was in full swing; the tent was full, and the evangelist was getting personal. He pointed to a known sinner in the front row. "Abner, come up here and join the Army of the Lord."*

*"Me, I already joined," declared Abner.*

*"Now just where did you join?"*

*"In the Baptist Church."*

*"You come on up here, Abner. You ain't in the Army, you are in the Navy."*

✠

The pretty Salvation Army lassie was singing on a street corner, trying to serve her Lord, when a cynical young man approached her, grinning. "Do you honestly believe," he sneered, "that Jonah spent three days and nights in the belly of a whale?"

"I don't know, sir," she admitted. "When I get to heaven I'll ask him."

"But suppose he isn't *in* heaven?"

"Then *you* ask him!"

✠

*"In times of trial," shouted one preacher from his pulpit, "what brings us the greatest comfort?"*

*From the back row a voice said: "An acquittal!"*

✠

"Why does the new minister read his sermon?" demanded a parishioner who was talking with a friend. "If *he* can't remember it, how does he expect us to?"

✠

In one town the day was hot. Very hot. The church was not refrigerated, and the people were sweating. The preacher preached on, and on, and on, and on. After nearly two hours he made an important point and shouted, "What more can I say?"

A voice from a back pew suggested: "Amen!"

✠

*George hadn't been in church lately, and when the minister met him on the street he said, "George, I hope you are not backsliding."*

*"No, sir, not exactly," George confessed. "But Preacher, my wife is learning to play the harp. And to tell you the truth, I'm not as keen about going to heaven now as I once was."*

The pastor was in fine form on Temperance Sunday. "Who," he shouted from his pulpit, "makes all the money in town? The saloonkeeper. Who lives in the finest house in town? The saloonkeeper. Whose wife has the finest furs, rides in the most expensive cars, travels to Europe? The saloonkeeper's. And my friends, who pays for all of this? YOU!"

At the church door a few minutes later, a smiling couple shook his hand, thanked him and said, "You made up our minds for us."

"Ah-h-h," beamed the pastor. "You have decided to give up liquor?"

"Oh, no, sir," the sweet lady explained, "we have decided to buy a saloon."

A churchman was talking about his new minister: "Six days a week he's invisible; on the seventh he's incomprehensible."

*Then, of course, there is the immortal story about that very self-conscious young man who became an usher in the highly fashionable Presbyterian Church, and was on duty for the first time. Stage fright beset him, before all those people. A wealthy old dowager marched imperiously down the aisle, and mistakenly sat down in the wrong pew.*

*The perspiring young usher hurried up to her, leaned close and whispered, "Mardon me, padam, you are occupewing the wrong pie. May I sew you to another sheet?"*

**72**

# 9.
# Wily Women

*"Women's* styles *may change," said one pas-tor, "but their designs remain the same."*

✠

The preacher trudged home very late for supper one night, and his wife chewed him out. Cried she, "Where on earth have you been for the last hour and a half?"

He was, of course, completely innocent. "I met Mrs. Hemingway on the sidewalk," he explained, wearily, "and I merely asked her how her married son was getting along. So she told me."

✠

*"Did they like my sermon?" the anxious young minister asked his wife, on their way home.*

*"I think so, dear," said she, tactfully. "At least they were all nodding."*

✠

Another pastor snapped at his wife, "Now, why did you ever purchase *that* new hat, dear? You know we couldn't afford it, not on *my* salary."

Mrs. Pastor replied, "But it was so pretty, I just couldn't resist it."

Pastor: "When you were tempted, why didn't you remember your Bible, and say, 'Get thee behind me, Satan!'"

Mrs. Pastor: "Oh, I did that. But Satan just exclaimed, 'My, how lovely it looks from the back!'"

The preacher was taken aback when he overheard this quick bit of talk between two ladies in the church hallway: "Listen carefully, Sue, because I can only tell this once. I promised not to repeat it."

✠

The distinguished Methodist preacher in Hollywood, Dr. Charles S. Kendall, conducts four identical services every Easter Sunday. One Easter in the middle of the third service, two well dressed ladies quietly got up and walked out. At the door the head usher asked them if one was ill. "Oh, no," said they, airily, "this is where we came in."

✠

*In one Grand Rapids church the worshipers did not maintain a strict silence until the opening organ music began, and even then they would finish their normal conversations. One morning the subdued murmur of greetings and talk was more pronounced than usual. When the organ music started the talk continued, naturally in a somewhat louder tone. In fact, one good lady had to raise her voice several levels to make her pew neighbor understand her. The choir filed in, the ministers took their seats, and the organ played on.*

*Suddenly the organ stopped. And in the quick hush, loud enough to be heard all over the church, came the tag end of the lady's discourse:* ". . . but I always whip the egg whites first."

✠

"Our church should be air conditioned," snapped Mrs. Lincoln. "It is unhealthy for people to sleep in a stuffy room."

Another preacher's wife was sniping at her husband: "I notice by this magazine article that men tend to become bald much more than women, because of the intense activity of their brains."

"Yes," the preacher sniped back, "and women can't raise beards because of the intense activity of their chins."

✛

*The baker suddenly had an order come in by telephone at four o'clock.*

*"Oh, Mr. Morris," the lady gushed, "I promised to take two dozen cup cakes to the church supper tonight and I simply haven't the time to bake them."*

*"I'll rush some out for you, ma'am."*

*"Oh, thank you! And be sure to make them look sloppy, please. That's how they would look if I had really baked them myself."*

✛

Church dinners are questionable at best. They run too much to meat loaf with cornflake filling, served on paper plates set on sawhorse-supported tables covered with unrolled wrapping paper, all on the mistaken premise that because it's in the church the "sociable" can be substandard. Even the drinks can be downscale. . . .

"This coffee is as weak as water!" snarled Deacon Jones at the church supper.

"Sh-h-h," cautioned his wife Maria. "You'll hurt somebody's feelings. It's my own Circle serving it tonight. Besides that, it's tea."

Up came another lady just then with her pot and said, "Deacon, may I pour you some more hot chocolate?"

Our preacher made me chairman of a committee to plan our church's 75th anniversary celebration, and I got the publicity off to a good start. I simply told each of our five Sewing Circles that each of the others thought they could handle publicity for the celebration without help.

✠

Some members of the church Sewing Circle were walking along the sidewalk and came to a store with a sign that read: LADIES READY-TO-WEAR CLOTHES. Firm-lipped Mrs. Hortense Goodnick snapped, "It's about time!"

✠

*A certain bishop was expected to preach in a small-town church. He was to arrive on a Saturday evening, and had planned to stay overnight in the local minister's home. The minister was to take him to a restaurant for dinner. But the train was delayed, and when the bishop finally got in, the restaurant was closed. So the minister took him home, explained the situation to his wife, and asked her to fix dinner for him.*

*While they waited, the bishop said he was tired. The minister suggested he go up to his own bedroom, put on his host's bedroom slippers, and make himself comfortable.*

*The minister's wife, unaware of this arrangement, also went up to their bedroom by way of the back stairs, entering the room from another door. Seeing the bent-over figure donning slippers, she slapped him heartily on his upturned posterior and said, "That's for bringing the bishop home to dinner."*

*In Dallas the very distinguished Dr. G..........
was completely indifferent to girth control, until one
week he discovered to his horror that his overcoat
was getting tighter each day, and by Friday wouldn't
button in the middle at all.*

*He started jogging, joined a YMCA health class,
went on strict diet and lost nearly forty pounds. Later he learned his two loyal secretaries had quietly
moved the coat buttons over one inch every day for
that one week.*

✠

Seems there was quite a hassle down at the church
kitchen last Wednesday night. Half the ladies pre-
paring the refreshments wanted rye bread in the
sandwiches, and half wanted whole wheat. What
they needed, it seems, was somebody to give in, such
as husbands.

✠

"When it comes to spreading gossip,"
mused the experienced pastor, "the female
of the species is much faster than the
mail."

✠

One of those too talkative women happened to go
walking down by the lake, and came across her pastor and a deacon, fishing. Moreover, they had a
string of fish.

"Aren't you men ashamed!" she scolded. "A deacon and a minister, cruelly putting hooks into helpless
fish. You might better be occupied doing good works.
Why, look, even now, parson, you are holding a helpless fish in your hand."

"Perhaps you are right, sister," the minister nodded. "But if this fish had had the sense to keep his mouth shut, he wouldn't be here."

✠

In Detroit the sight-seeing bus was rolling along, and a lady was much excited as the driver pointed out places of interest.

"Right yonder," said he, "is the Dodge home."

"John Dodge?" asked the eager lady.

"No, Horace Dodge."

Out Jefferson Avenue, the driver said, "On the right you see the Ford home."

"Henry Ford?" the lady asked.

"No, Edsel Ford."

The bus rolled on out Jefferson Avenue, and presently the driver said, "On our left, we have the Christ Church."

When no comment was heard, the driver turned around and said, "Go ahead, lady, you can't be wrong all the time."

✠

*The distinguished Rev. Elmer Straitlace was asked to be one of the judges at the local dog show, and he accepted. Arriving there, he was shocked at the way most of the girl exhibitors had dressed.*

*"It is an outrage!" he stormed to a person near him. "Just look at that creature with the wolfhound, for example. Hair cut too close. Wearing trousers. Cigarette dangling. Is it a boy or a girl?"*

*The listener said, "It's a girl. She's my daughter."*

*"Well, you must forgive me, then," the preacher apologized. "I never would have guessed that you were her father."*

*"I'm not. I'm her mother."*

**78**

A tired clergyman was at home resting. But, through the window he saw a woman approaching his door, one of those too talkative pests he was not anxious to greet. He said to his wife, "I'll just duck upstairs and wait until she goes away."

An hour passed, then he tiptoed to the stair landing and listened. Not a sound. He was very pleased, so he started clumping down calling loudly to his wife, "Well, my dear, so you got rid of that old bore at last."

The next moment he heard the voice of the same woman caller, and she couldn't possibly have missed hearing him. Two steps down, he saw them both staring up at him. It seemed truly a crisis moment.

But the wise Mrs. Preacher simply answered: "Yes, dear, *she* went away over an hour ago. But here is Mrs. Blank come to call,and I'm sure you'll be glad to greet *her*."

✠

*In Laguna Beach, California, a Christian Science member attended the Presbyterian church where Dr. Dallas Turner preached. After a few weeks some good member asked the woman if she wouldn't like Dr. Turner to call.*

*"I should say not," the woman exclaimed. "I don't want him hounding me about joining his church. Furthermore, I would like you to know I don't believe a thing he says. But I just* love *the way he says it!"*

✠

"I can remember," mused the elderly pastor, "when a wife asked her husband *what* he wanted to eat, instead of *where*."

The lady had gone to her pastor for guidance. Said she, "How can I get my husband to discuss his business affairs with me?"

Replied the preacher: "Simply ask him when he intends to buy a new car."

✠

*One dear lady grasped the new minister's hand at the door after his first sermon and gushed, "Oh, Dr. Smith, welcome again! We simply didn't know what sin was until you arrived."*

✠

A new and pretty girl who was not a member came to church, and after service she was drinking coffee with the rest in the patio. Kindly Rev. Tom Barker, married and a father, thought to welcome her. So he got her name, told her his, thanked her for coming, then asked, "And where do you live?"

Rather suspicious, and very serious, she lifted big blue eyes to his and told him: "I already got a fella."

✠

"A misunderstood wife," suggested the Rev. Scott Westmoreland, "is the one who telephoned her husband to bring home a quart of lacquer."

✠

Whatever other problems poor Adam may have faced, he at least never had to listen to Eve complain about other women having finer clothes than she.